I0021558

Copyright © 2023 by Snowie Garys

All rights reserved. No part of this publication may be reproduced, distributed, or transmitted in any form or by any means, including photocopying, recording, or other electronic or mechanical methods, without the prior written permission of the publisher, except in the case of brief quotations embodied in critical reviews and certain other noncommercial uses permitted by copyright law.

INTRODUCTION TO DIGITAL MARKETING

Table of Contents

CHAPTER 1

INTRODUCTION

The field of marketing has experienced a significant shift due to the prevalence of technology and connectivity in today's world. Digital Marketing is the driving force behind this transformation. As we continue to navigate through this digital era, it's becoming more and more clear that the ability to comprehend and utilize digital marketing is not just beneficial but a necessity for both businesses and individuals.

1. Definition of Digital Marketing

At its substance, Computerized Showcasing addresses a change in outlook on how items and administrations are advanced, utilizing advanced channels and advancements to reach and draw in interest groups. From web-based entertainment stages and web crawlers to email and then some, computerized promoting envelops a huge swath of techniques pointed toward making significant associations and encouraging brand permeability in the web-based circle. This digital book intends to demystify the complexities of computerized showcasing, giving a far-reaching investigation of its essential standards and procedures.

2. Evolution and Significance of Digital Marketing

The story of digital marketing's evolution is an intriguing one that reflects the rapid progress of technology. From its modest origins as static banner ads to the advanced, data-driven campaigns of today, digital marketing has become a powerful driving force behind business growth and customer engagement. In this section, we will examine the historical context of digital marketing, uncovering its transformative journey and highlighting the pivotal moments that have shaped its significance in the modern business world.

3. Overview of the Digital Landscape

To navigate the world of digital marketing, one must first understand the vast and ever-changing digital landscape. This section serves as a compass, offering readers a panoramic view of the diverse channels, platforms, and technologies that constitute the digital marketing ecosystem. From the social media realms to the intricacies of search engine optimization and the expanding horizons of emerging technologies, we will embark on a journey that illuminates the expansive canvas upon which digital marketing strategies are crafted.

As we begin our journey into the world of digital marketing, let's envision a roadmap that will provide you with the knowledge, tools, and strategies necessary to thrive in the digital realm. The pages that follow will unravel the intricacies of each facet, offering not only theoretical insights but also practical guidance to help you on your digital marketing journey. Welcome to the Introduction to Digital Marketing, your gateway to the dynamic world where innovation, connectivity, and strategic prowess converge to redefine the way we connect, communicate, and captivate audiences in the digital era.

CHAPTER 2

Fundamentals of Digital Marketing

In the ever-evolving tapestry of the digital age, understanding the core principles that underpin successful marketing is the cornerstone of navigating the complex landscape of digital marketing. As we delve into the second chapter of "Introduction to Digital Marketing," let's unravel the fundamental principles, distinguish the nuances between traditional and digital marketing, and explore the key components that shape an effective digital marketing strategy.

1. The Core Principles of Marketing in the Digital Age

1.1 Customer-Centricity

In the digital realm, success hinges on understanding and addressing the needs of your audience. Customer-centricity remains a timeless principle, but in the digital age, the ability to personalize interactions and tailor content to individual preferences takes center stage.

1.2 Data-Driven Decision Making

Digital marketing is synonymous with data. The ability to gather, analyze, and derive actionable insights from data empowers marketers to make informed decisions. In this section, we explore how data-driven approaches enhance campaign efficiency and effectiveness.

1.3 Continuous Adaptation

The computerized scene is continually advancing, with arising patterns and advancements. It's critical to stay adaptable and have a mentality of constant transformation to remain ahead. We talk about methodologies for embracing change and utilizing new open doors.

2. Distinctions Between Traditional and Digital Marketing

2.1 Interaction vs. Interruption

Traditional marketing often involves interrupting the consumer's experience (e.g., TV ads), while digital marketing provides opportunities for interactive engagement. We examine how the shift from interruption to interaction reshapes the marketing paradigm.

7

2.2 Reach and Targeting Precision

One of the striking differentiations is the capacity to draw in your crowd progressively and get moment criticism. We examine what this continuous communication means for procedure refinement and client connections

2.3 Real-Time Engagement and Feedback

One of the striking differentiations is the capacity to draw in your crowd progressively and get moment criticism. We examine what this continuous communication means for procedure refinement and client connections.

3. Key Components of a Successful Digital Marketing Strategy

3.1 Clear Objectives and KPIs

A successful digital marketing strategy begins with clear, measurable objectives. We guide you through the process of defining goals and selecting key performance indicators (KPIs) aligned with your business objectives.

3.2 Comprehensive Audience Analysis

Understanding your target audience is paramount. We delve into the tools and methods for conducting audience analysis to tailor your messaging and approach effectively.

3.3 Multi-Channel Integration

Digital marketing spans multiple channels. Learn how to harmonize efforts across platforms, ensuring a cohesive and seamless experience for your audience.

3.4 Content Strategy and Storytelling

Quality content is the linchpin of digital marketing success. This section explores how to craft a compelling content strategy and the art of storytelling to captivate your audience.

As we navigate the fundamentals of digital marketing, remember that mastery of these principles lays the groundwork for the chapters to come. Embrace the shift in mindset, adapt to the digital landscape, and forge a path towards creating impactful, customer-centric campaigns. Welcome to the heart of digital marketing mastery.

CHAPTER 3

Digital Marketing Channels

In the vast tapestry of digital marketing, success lies in mastering the art of navigating diverse channels strategically. Chapter III of "Introduction to Digital Marketing" dives deep into the key channels that shape online engagement, brand visibility, and audience interaction. Let's explore the dynamic realms of Social Media Marketing, Search Engine Optimization (SEO), Email Marketing, and Pay-Per-Click (PPC) Advertising.

1. Social Media Marketing

1.1 Strategies for Major Platforms

Unravel the nuances of crafting effective strategies on major social media platforms – Facebook, Instagram, Twitter, and LinkedIn. Discover the unique opportunities and best practices for audience engagement on each platform.

1.2 Building and Engaging an Audience

Building a loyal social media following is an art. Learn how to create meaningful connections, foster engagement, and cultivate a community around your brand. Dive into tactics that transform casual followers into brand advocates.

2. Search Engine Optimization (SEO)

2.1 Basics of SEO

Unlock the mysteries of SEO by delving into its fundamental principles. From on-page optimization to keyword research, understand the core elements that influence search engine rankings.

2.2 On-Page and Off-Page Optimization

Explore the complexities of on-page and off-page Search engine optimization methods. Uncover procedures to improve your site's permeability in list items and construct a hearty web-based presence.

2.3 SEO Tools and Best Practices

Explore a toolkit of SEO resources and best practices. From Google Analytics to keyword research tools, we guide you through the essential tools that empower your SEO endeavors.

3. Email Marketing

3.1 Building and Maintaining Email Lists

Discover the art of building an engaged subscriber base. From lead generation to list segmentation, explore strategies to cultivate a quality email list.

3.2 Crafting Effective Email Campaigns

Ace the specialty of creating convincing email crusades. From titles to invigorate buttons, figure out how to spellbind your crowd and drive wanted activities through email.

3.3 Email Marketing Analytics

Unearth the power of email marketing analytics. Dive into metrics that matter and gain insights into recipient behavior to continually refine your email marketing strategy.

4. Pay-Per-Click (PPC) Advertising

4.1 Overview of PPC

Demystify the world of Pay-Per-Click advertising. Understand the core concepts, bidding strategies, and ad formats that define successful PPC campaigns.

4.2 Google Ads and Other Platforms

Embark on a journey through the Google Ads platform and explore other popular PPC advertising platforms. Learn how to navigate interfaces, set budgets, and create compelling ad content.

4.3 Ad Creation and Optimization

Making a powerful promotion is workmanship. Dig into the standards of promotion creation and enhancement, guaranteeing your missions augment permeability and profit from the venture.

As we adventure through the computerized promoting channels, imagine your image thriving across stages. Each channel offers a remarkable chance to interface, draw in, permeability, and convert. Welcome to the powerful reality where advanced channels become the conductors of your

image's story.

CHAPTER 5

Content Marketing

Welcome to the heart of storytelling in the digital realm. Chapter IV of "Introduction to Digital Marketing" delves into the intricate world of Content Marketing. In this chapter, we unravel the essence, creation, distribution, and analytics of content, exploring how this art form shapes brand narratives and fosters audience connections.

1. Definition and Importance of Content Marketing

1.1 Crafting a Definition

Leave on an excursion to grasp the center meaning of content showcasing. Investigate how it rises above simple advancement to turn into a vehicle for esteem conveyance and crowd commitment.

1.2 Unveiling its Importance

Delve into the pivotal role content marketing plays in the digital landscape. From building brand authority to nurturing customer relationships, uncover the significance of content as the linchpin of digital strategy.

2. Creating Valuable and Engaging Content

2.1 The Art of Storytelling

Discover the transformative power of storytelling. Uncover techniques to weave narratives that resonate with your audience, creating a lasting impact and forging emotional connections.

2.2 Tailoring Content to Your Audience

Understand your audience's needs, preferences, and pain points. Learn how to tailor content that speaks directly to your target demographic, enhancing engagement and brand loyalty.

3. Content Distribution Strategies

3.1 Selecting Platforms Wisely

Navigate the multitude of content distribution platforms. From social media channels to blogs and beyond, discern the ideal platforms that align with your brand and target audience.

3.2 Maximizing Reach Through SEO

Explore how content and SEO intersect. Unearth strategies to optimize your content for search engines, ensuring your creations reach a wider audience organically.

3.3 Embracing Multichannel Distribution

Master the art of multichannel distribution. Understand how to leverage various platforms simultaneously to amplify your content's reach and impact.

4. Content Marketing Analytics

4.1 Defining Key Metrics

Navigate the realm of content marketing analytics by understanding key performance indicators (KPIs). Identify metrics that measure engagement, conversion, and overall content effectiveness.

4.2 Tools for Analysis

Explore a toolkit of analytics tools. From Google Analytics to social media insights, discover resources that empower you to assess the performance of your content marketing efforts.

4.3 Iterating Based on Insights

Transform data into action. Learn how to interpret analytics insights and use them to refine your content strategy continuously. Embrace a cycle of creation, analysis, and optimization.

As we traverse the realm of content marketing, envision your brand's story unfolding in the hearts and minds of your audience. Each piece of content becomes a brushstroke, contributing to the masterpiece of your digital presence. Welcome to the transformative world where storytelling transcends, engages, and endures.

CHAPTER 5

Analytics and Data-Driven Marketing

Step into the realm of precision and insight as Chapter V of "Introduction to Digital Marketing" navigates the transformative landscape of Analytics and Data-Driven Marketing. In this chapter, we unravel the significance of web analytics, explore key metrics for gauging digital marketing success, delve into powerful data analysis tools, and discover the art of implementing decisions driven by data.

1. Introduction to Web Analytics

1.1 Decoding the Role of Web Analytics

Leave on an excursion into the universe of web investigation. Comprehend how this crucial device catches and deciphers client conduct on your computerized resources, giving a window into the viability of your internet-based presence.

1.2 The Power of Data-Driven Insights

Explore how web analytics transforms raw data into actionable insights. From page views to user demographics, grasp the metrics that illuminate user engagement and inform strategic decisions.

2. Key Metrics for Measuring Digital Marketing Success

2.1 Traffic and Audience Metrics

Dive into the core metrics that measure the influx and behavior of your digital audience. Understand the significance of metrics such as website visits, unique visitors, and bounce rates in assessing overall traffic quality.

2.2 Conversion Metrics

Unlock the secrets behind conversion metrics. From click-through rates to conversion rates, explore how these metrics quantify the effectiveness of your digital marketing efforts in turning visitors into customers.

2.3 Engagement Metrics

Delve into metrics that gauge user engagement. Discover how time on the page, social media interactions, and comments contribute to a holistic understanding of audience involvement.

3. Tools for Data Analysis and Interpretation

3.1 Google Analytics and Beyond

Uncover the potential of Google Analytics as a cornerstone for data analysis. Explore additional tools and platforms that complement your analytics toolkit, offering nuanced insights into various aspects of your digital presence.

3.2 Social Media Insights

Navigate the landscape of social media analytics. From Facebook Insights to Twitter Analytics, learn how to extract valuable data from social platforms to refine your social media marketing strategy.

4. Implementing Data-Driven Decisions

4.1 Interpreting Insights into Action

Transforming data into actionable strategies is an art. Explore methodologies for interpreting analytics insights and making informed decisions that enhance your digital marketing campaigns.

4.2 A/B Testing and Iterative Improvement

Delve into the world of A/B testing. Understand how experimentation and iterative improvement based on data-driven insights can optimize your digital marketing efforts over time.

4.3 Establishing a Culture of Data-Driven Decision Making

Embark on the journey of cultivating a culture that values and leverages data. Learn how to foster an environment where insights gleaned from analytics become integral to every decision in your digital marketing strategy.

As we navigate the landscape of data-driven marketing, envision a future where every click, interaction, and engagement contributes to a finely tuned symphony of strategy. Welcome to the transformative power of analytics – the compass guiding your digital journey toward precision and success.

CHAPTER 6

Mobile Marketing

As our digital footprint expands into the palms of our hands, Chapter VI of "Introduction to Digital Marketing" unveils the dynamic universe of Mobile Marketing. In this chapter, we explore strategies that embrace the mobile-first paradigm, uncover the intricacies of app marketing and optimization, and delve into the realms of SMS marketing and mobile advertising.

1. Mobile-Friendly Strategies

1.1 Navigating the Mobile-First Landscape

Understand the critical importance of mobile-friendly strategies in a world where smartphones are ubiquitous. Explore responsive design, user-friendly interfaces, and other essentials to ensure a seamless mobile experience for your audience.

1.2 Mobile SEO Best Practices

Dive into the specifics of mobile Search Engine Optimization (SEO). Learn how to optimize your digital assets for mobile search, ensuring visibility and engagement in a mobile-first world.

2. App Marketing and Optimization

2.1 Crafting a Stellar App Marketing Strategy

Embark on the journey of promoting and driving downloads for your mobile application. Explore strategies that capture attention, highlight unique selling propositions, and encourage users to install your app.

2.2 App Store Optimization (ASO)

Unlock the secrets of App Store Optimization. From keyword optimization to compelling visuals, discover how to position your app for success within crowded app marketplaces.

2.3 Retention Strategies

Building an app is only the beginning. Explore strategies for retaining users and fostering long-term engagement. From push notifications to in-app messaging, learn how to keep your app users coming back.

3. SMS Marketing and Mobile Advertising

3.1 The Power of SMS Marketing

Dig into the immediate and individual domain of SMS showcasing. Investigate best practices for making convincing SMS crusades that enrapture your crowd and drive wanted activities.

3.2 Mobile Advertising Strategies

Investigate the varying scene of flexible advancing. From show ads to in-application advancements, research the scope of game plans available and grasp how to accommodate your publicizing procedure to versatile stages.

3.3 Location-Based Marketing

Uncover the potential of location-based marketing in the mobile space. Explore how geotargeting and location-based services can enhance the relevance and impact of your mobile marketing campaigns.

As we immerse ourselves in the realm of mobile marketing, envision a landscape where every touchpoint, notification, and interaction is optimized for the mobile user. Welcome to the era where mobile devices are not just tools but gateways to immersive and personalized brand experiences. Embrace the power of mobile marketing to connect with your audience anytime, anywhere.

CHAPTER 7

Emerging Trends and Technologies

In the always-advancing scene of computerized advertising, Section VII of "Introduction to Digital Marketing" makes the way for the state-of-the-art outskirts where development and innovation join. Investigate the groundbreaking capability of Man-made reasoning, the ascent of Voice Inquiry Improvement, the vivid encounters presented by Expanded Reality (AR) and Computer-generated Reality (VR), and the decentralized potential outcomes brought by Blockchain in the domain of advanced showcasing.

1. Artificial Intelligence in Digital Marketing

1.1 Understanding AI's Role

Dig into the transformative role of Artificial Intelligence (AI) in reshaping digital marketing. Explore how AI-powered tools and algorithms enhance personalization, automation, and predictive analytics, revolutionizing the way brands connect with their audience.

1.2 AI-Driven Personalization

Uncover the power of AI in crafting personalized experiences for users. From dynamic content recommendations to tailored messaging, explore how AI refines and customizes marketing strategies.

1.3 Predictive Analytics and Machine Learning

Navigate the landscape of predictive analytics and machine learning. Learn how AI algorithms analyze vast datasets to forecast trends, optimize campaigns, and enhance decision-making processes in digital marketing.

2. Voice Search Optimization

2.1 The Rise of Voice Search

Explore the surge in voice-activated searches and the impact on digital marketing. Understand how optimizing for voice search differs from traditional SEO strategies and the importance of adapting to this evolving trend.

2.2 Strategies for Voice Search Optimization

Delve into actionable strategies for optimizing content and campaigns for voice search. From conversational keywords to local search considerations, uncover the nuances of an effective voice search optimization strategy.

3. Augmented Reality (AR) and Virtual Reality (VR)

3.1 Immersive Experiences with AR

Embark on a journey into the world of Augmented Reality. Explore how AR enhances user experiences by overlaying digital elements in the real world, opening new possibilities for interactive and engaging marketing campaigns.

3.2 Virtual Reality's Impact on Engagement

Delve into the immersive realm of Virtual Reality. Discover how VR transports users to virtual environments, offering brands the opportunity to create memorable and impactful marketing experiences.

4. Blockchain in Digital Marketing

4.1 Decentralization and Transparency

Uncover the potential of blockchain technology in fostering decentralization and transparency within digital marketing. Explore how blockchain can mitigate fraud, enhance security, and provide a verifiable record of transactions.

4.2 Smart Contracts and Consumer Trust

Navigate the concept of smart contracts in digital marketing. Understand how self-executing contracts built on blockchain technology can streamline processes, build trust, and enhance transparency in marketing transactions.

As we explore these emerging trends and technologies, envision a future where AI optimizes, voice search transforms, augmented and virtual reality captivates, and blockchain revolutionizes the landscape of digital marketing. Welcome to the forefront of innovation, where the intersection of technology and marketing shapes the future of digital engagement.

CHAPTER 8

Digital Marketing Tools and Resources

In the steadily advancing field of computerized advertising, Part VIII of "Introduction to Digital Marketing" makes the way for a variety of fundamental apparatuses and assets. Find the devices that engage computerized advertisers, track down dependable assets to keep up to date with industry drifts, and figure out how to construct a strong advanced showcasing tool stash.

1. Overview of Essential Tools for Digital Marketers

1.1 Analytics and Data Insights

Explore tools that unravel the intricacies of data. From Google Analytics for website metrics to social media analytics platforms, understand how these tools provide the data-driven insights necessary for informed decision-making.

1.2 Content Creation and Management

Delve into content creation and management tools. From graphic design platforms to content calendars and collaboration tools, discover resources that streamline the content creation process.

1.3 Social Media Management

Explore the unique universe of online entertainment and the executive's instruments. Investigate stages that work with planning, checking, and commitment across different web-based entertainment channels to enhance your virtual entertainment procedure.

1.4 SEO and Keyword Research

Uncover the tools essential for SEO and keyword research. From keyword planners to backlink analysis tools, understand how these resources contribute to optimizing your digital presence for search engines.

2. Resources for Staying Updated on Industry Trends

2.1 Industry Blogs and Websites

Discover reputable blogs and websites that serve as hubs for industry insights. From Moz to HubSpot, explore platforms that provide up-to-date articles, case studies, and analyses on digital marketing trends.

2.2 Podcasts and Webinars

Embark on an auditory exploration of digital marketing trends through podcasts and webinars. Uncover resources that deliver expert interviews, discussions, and insights to keep you informed while on the go.

2.3 Online Courses and Certifications

Explore the world of continuous learning through online courses and certifications. Platforms like Coursera and LinkedIn Learning offer courses on various digital marketing topics, allowing you to deepen your knowledge and skills.

3. Building a Digital Marketing Toolkit

3.1 Assessing Your Needs

Understand the specific needs of your digital marketing strategy. Whether it's analytics, social media, or content creation, tailor your toolkit to address your unique goals and challenges.

3.2 Integration and Compatibility

Explore how different tools can work together seamlessly. Building a toolkit that integrates with your existing systems ensures a cohesive and efficient workflow.

3.3 Budget Considerations

Navigate the landscape of free and paid tools. While some essential tools offer free versions, others may require an investment. Consider your budget and prioritize tools that align with your financial constraints.

3.4 Scalability

Anticipate growth in your digital marketing efforts. Choose tools that are scalable and adaptable to the evolving needs of your strategy as your brand expands and diversifies.

As you immerse yourself in the world of digital marketing tools and resources, envision a toolkit that empowers your strategies, keeps you informed, and fosters continuous growth. Welcome to the dynamic realm where the right tools and resources become the catalysts for successful digital marketing endeavors.

CHAPTER 9

Case Studies

Chapter IX of "Introduction to Digital Marketing" immerses you in the real-world narratives of successful digital marketing campaigns. Journey through compelling case studies that illustrate the application of strategies across various industries. Uncover the challenges faced by these campaigns and explore the innovative solutions that propelled them to success.

1. Real-world examples of Successful Digital Marketing Campaigns

1.1 Nike's "Dream Crazy" Campaign

Explore the iconic "Dream Crazy" campaign by Nike, featuring Colin Kaepernick. Uncover how this socially impactful campaign leveraged bold storytelling and strategic use of social media to resonate with audiences globally, resulting in increased brand loyalty and market share.

1.2 Airbnb's "Live There" Campaign

Dive into the "Live There" campaign by Airbnb, showcasing immersive travel experiences. Understand how Airbnb utilized user-generated content and a strategic blend of digital channels to connect with its community, driving engagement and expanding its user base.

1.3 Coca-Cola's "Share a Coke" Campaign

Discover the "Share a Coke" campaign by Coca-Cola, where personalized packaging became a global sensation. Explore how this campaign utilized social media, user participation, and personalized content to create a viral marketing phenomenon and boost sales.

2. Analysis of Challenges and Solutions

2.1 Overcoming Audience Saturation

Explore how brands addressed the challenge of audience saturation. Dive into strategies employed to break through the digital noise and capture the attention of audiences inundated with information.

2.2 Navigating Evolving Algorithms

Uncover how computerized showcasing efforts adjusted to changing calculations via web-based entertainment stages and web indexes. Inspect the strategies used to keep up with permeability and viability during algorithmic movements.

2.3 Privacy Concerns and Data Security

Delve into cases where privacy concerns and data security posed challenges to digital marketing efforts. Explore the solutions employed to build and maintain trust, ensuring continued consumer engagement in an era of heightened data sensitivity.

2.4 Adapting to Technological Advancements

Explore how digital marketers navigated the rapid evolution of technology. Understand the challenges presented by emerging trends and technologies and the innovative solutions that allowed campaigns to stay ahead of the curve.

As we explore these case studies, envision the application of successful strategies to your digital marketing endeavors. Each case study serves as a beacon of inspiration and a source of valuable lessons, guiding you through the complexities and triumphs of real-world digital marketing challenges.

Welcome to the immersive world where theory meets reality, and strategic innovation paves the way for digital marketing success.

CHAPTER 10

Conclusion

As we reach the final chapter of "Introduction to Digital Marketing," let's embark on a reflective journey, summarizing key concepts and laying the groundwork for your ongoing exploration and mastery of the dynamic realm of digital marketing.

1. Recap of Key Concepts

1.1 The Essence of Digital Marketing

Reflect on the fundamental definition of digital marketing – the art and science of strategically engaging audiences through online channels. Grasp the significance of this transformative discipline in reshaping how businesses connect with their target demographic.

1.2 Core Principles

Recall the core principles that drive success in the digital age. From customer-centricity to data-driven decision-making and a mindset of continuous adaptation, internalize the foundational elements that underpin effective digital marketing strategies.

1.3 Digital Marketing Channels

Review the diverse channels explored – from the immersive landscapes of social media to the intricacies of SEO, email marketing, and PPC advertising. Each channel offers unique opportunities for engagement, conversion, and brand visibility.

1.4 Emerging Trends and Technologies

Recapture the excitement of emerging trends and technologies, from the transformative power of

artificial intelligence and voice search optimization
to the immersive experiences offered by augmented
and virtual reality, and the decentralized potential of
blockchain.

1.5 Case Studies

Revisit the real-world examples that showcased the
application of digital marketing strategies.
Understand the challenges faced by iconic
campaigns and the innovative solutions that
propelled them to success.

2. Encouragement for Further Exploration and Learning in Digital Marketing

2.1 Lifelong Learning

Computerized advertising is an always advancing
scene. Urge yourself to take on an outlook of deep-
rooted learning. The techniques and advances

examined in this book are only a glimpse of something larger. Remain inquisitive, remain hungry for information, and embrace the constant development of the advanced advertising domain.

2.2 Explore Specialized Areas

Computerized promotion is an immense field with particular specialties. Consider digging further into regions that line up with your inclinations and vocation objectives. Whether it's online entertainment promoting, Website design enhancement, information examination, or rising advancements, there is something else to learn and dominate.

2.3 Networking and Community

Join computerized advertising networks, go to gatherings, and draw in with experts in the field.

Organizing gives important experiences as well as opens ways for cooperation and mentorship. Encircle yourself with a local area that shares your enthusiasm for computerized promoting.

2.4 Hands-On Experience

Theory is valuable, but hands-on experience is irreplaceable. Implement the strategies you've learned, experiment with different tools, and analyze the results. Practical experience is a powerful teacher in the world of digital marketing.

2.5 Certification and Professional Development

Consider pursuing certifications in digital marketing to enhance your credibility and skill set. Many reputable organizations offer certification programs that validate your expertise and keep you up-to-date with industry best practices.

All in all, "Introduction to Digital Marketing" is only the start of your excursion into the astonishing and steadily developing universe of computerized showcasing. As you close this book, recollect that the computerized scene is dynamic, and achievement arrives at the individuals who are versatile, creative, and focused on continuous learning. Embrace the difficulties, commend the triumphs, and keep forming your computerized promoting aptitude. Welcome to a future loaded up with vast potential outcomes in the enrapturing domain of computerized showcasing.

CHAPTER 11

Appendices

As a comprehensive resource for digital marketers, the appendices chapter of "Introduction to Digital Marketing" provides additional tools and references to support your journey. Whether you're looking to clarify terminology, explore recommended reading, or pursue certification programs, these appendices are designed to be valuable companions to your digital marketing education.

1. Glossary of Digital Marketing Terms

1.1 A/B Testing

A technique for contrasting two variants of a site page or battle to figure out which performs better, giving experiences to streamlining.

1.2 Conversion Rate

The level of site guests who make an ideal move, like making a buy or finishing up a structure.

1.3 SERP (Search Engine Results Page)

The page is shown by a web search tool in light of a client's question, posting significant sites and content.

1.4 CTR (Click-Through Rate)

The level of individuals who click on a promotion or connection contrasted with the complete number of individuals who see it.

1.5 ROI (Return on Investment)

A metric that assesses the benefit of speculation is normally used to evaluate the viability of showcasing efforts.

1.6 UGC (User-Generated Content)

Content made by clients or clients instead of the actual brand is much of the time shared via virtual entertainment or integrated into advertising procedures.

This glossary gives a fast reference to computerized showcasing terms experienced all through the book, guaranteeing lucidity and understanding as you explore the advanced scene.

2. Recommended Reading and Resources

2.1 Books

- "Contagious: How to Build Word of Mouth in the Digital Age" by Jonah Berger

- "Everybody Writes: Your Go-To Guide to Creating Ridiculously Good Content" by Ann Handley

- "SEO for Dummies" by Peter Kent

2.2 Blogs and Websites

- Moz (https://moz.com/blog)

- HubSpot Blog (https://blog.hubspot.com)

- Neil Patel's Blog (https://neilpatel.com/blog)

2.3 Podcasts

- "Marketing School" by Neil Patel & Eric Siu

- "The Social Media Marketing Podcast" by Michael Stelzner

- "The GaryVee Audio Experience" by Gary Vaynerchuk

Explore these recommended resources to deepen your knowledge, stay updated on industry trends, and gain insights from thought leaders in the field.

3. Digital Marketing Certification Programs

3.1 Google Ads Certification

Earn recognition for your proficiency in Google Ads and demonstrate your ability to create effective online advertising campaigns.

3.2 HubSpot Content Marketing Certification

Validate your expertise in content marketing with HubSpot's certification program, covering content creation, strategy, and promotion.

3.3 Facebook Blueprint Certification

Demonstrate your mastery of Facebook advertising with the Blueprint Certification, showcasing your skills in creating and optimizing ad campaigns.

3.4 Google Analytics Individual Qualification (GAIQ)

Become certified in Google Analytics, showcasing your ability to use the platform to analyze data and make informed decisions.

These certification programs offer formal recognition of your digital marketing skills and can enhance your credibility in the professional landscape.

As you explore these appendices, consider them as valuable companions in your ongoing journey through the dynamic and ever-evolving realm of digital marketing. Each resource is designed to support your learning, provide clarity, and empower you as you navigate the exciting landscape of digital marketing.

www.ingramcontent.com/pod-product-compliance
Lightning Source LLC
Chambersburg PA
CBHW061050050326
40690CB00012B/2571